A Visit to N

By Jenna Lee Gleisner

SPARKS

Picture Glossary

This is my school.

It is big.

school

This is my school.

It has my classroom.

classroom

This is my school.

It has desks.

desk

This is my school.

It has a library.

library

This is my school.

It has a gym.

gym

This is my school.

It has a lunchroom.

lunchroom

Do You Know?

What room is this in the school?

classroom

library

gym

lunchroom